D1002710

BECOMING FULLY HUMAN

a biblical perspective

WALTER VOGELS

BECOMING FULLY HUMAN

a biblical perspective

Novalis/Wood Lake Books

Biblical quotations are from *The Jerusalem Bible*.

Cover and design: Gilles Lépine

© 1988 Novalis, Saint Paul University, Ottawa, Canada

Novalis
P. O. Box 9700, Terminal
Ottawa, Ontario K1G 4B4

Wood Lake Books
P. O. Box 700
Winfield, British Columbia VOH 2C0

ISBN 2-89088-367-1 (Novalis)
ISBN 0-919599-66-4 (Wood Lake Books)

Printed in Canada

CONTENTS

Introduction 7

Chapter One: Openness to God 15
  1. Search................................ 18
  2. Acceptance.......................... 27
  3. Faithfulness 34
  4. Freedom 42

Chapter Two: Solidarity with Others 55
  1. Admiration 58
  2. Understanding 64
  3. Reconciliation 70

Chapter Three: Respect for Nature......... 77
  1. Belonging 80
  2. Development......................... 86
  3. Preservation........................ 93

Conclusion 99
Suggested Readings......................... 102

INTRODUCTION

The Bible is a truly extraordinary book. It expresses people's life experiences and it also invites us to enter into these experiences. As such the Bible was not written simply to be read, but to be lived.

But what does this imply for us? How can we read the Bible with a view to living it? There are different ways of answering this question. We'll begin by examining two common ones: using proof texts to deal with tough moral dilemmas, and adopting biblical characters as role models for our behaviour. We'll then move on to a third approach which stresses the discovery of life principles which give meaning and direction to human life.

Looking for answers

Nowadays, it seems, many people are confused when it comes to moral issues. The social sciences have shed a great deal of light on what makes us tick as human beings, and the medical sciences have contributed immensely to our knowledge of the human body and how it functions. These scientific advances, along with rapid social change, have thrown into question some of our long held and cherished notions of what constitues right and wrong. Just think about all those debates concerning abortion or euthanasia! The result is that many of us feel at loose ends and aren't quite sure what to think. What was once black and white in the area of morality has suddenly turned grey!

So many people are turning to the Bible in hopes of finding those black and white answers. But they aren't necessarily there. Let me give you an example. In the past, moral theologians offered convincing arguments based on Scripture to condemn practices such as homosexuality. To the surprise of the faithful, that same Bible is suddenly being used to prove that there is nothing wrong with homosexuality. In fact, some theologians maintain that certain biblical texts are very positive about same sex friendships: David loved Jonathan, and Jesus had a disciple he loved.

The same thing is happening with other difficult moral issues. In the past the Bible was used to condemn certain activities, and now it's being used to provide a seal of approval. Each side quotes an appropriate text to prove its point and to serve its own purposes. Clearly, this selective use of texts is the wrong way to go about things — the Bible is not a manual of moral theology.

Following the leader

Another way of using the Bible, and one that's just as misleading, is to see it as a compendium of virtues and saints to imitate.

Take Abraham, for instance. He is often considered a model of hospitality. When three strangers came to visit, he welcomed them warmly. His generous attitude is quite the reverse of the selfish individualism so noticeable in our society today. Hence, he is a good example for us to follow, right? Before jumping to conclusions, maybe we should read the text a little more carefully. You may end up with a few reservations about Abraham's so-called hospitality. After ordering water brought to his visitors: "Abraham hastened to the tent to find Sarah. 'Hurry,' he said, 'knead three bushels of flour and make loaves.' Then running to the cattle Abraham took a fine and tender calf and gave it to the servant, who hurried to prepare it" (Genesis 18: 6-7).

Practising hospitality is rather easy when others have to do all the work. This story will not impress women very much. Is this a wife's role? Abraham treats Sarah exactly as he treats his servants, and she isn't even invited to share in the meal — she's stuck in the kitchen.

But this isn't the only event that prevents the patriarch from being a model of all possible virtues. Consider this example:

On the threshold of Egypt he (Abram) said to his wife Sarai, ''Listen! I know that you are a beautiful woman. When the Egyptians see you they will say, 'That is his wife,' and they will kill me but spare you. Tell them you are my sister, so that they may treat me well because of you and spare my life out of regard for you.'' (Genesis 12:11-13)

No matter what custom may have been behind this story, no matter how clever you may think Abraham was, his behaviour was anything but exemplary. Women especially find it disgusting and offensive.

Here's another incident which has rather questionable ethical implications for us today:

Abram's wife Sarai had borne him no child, but she had an Egyptian maidservant named Hagar.

10

So Sarai said to Abram, "Listen, now! Since Yahweh has kept me from having children, go to my slave-girl. Perhaps I shall get children through her." Abram agreed to what Sarai had said. (Genesis 16:1-2)

Similar customs still exist in certain cultures — we could even compare this practice to motherhood by proxy in the West. But it seems rather doubtful that we have to imitate the example of Abraham to live biblically.

These are just three events in the life of one person, but they serve to demonstrate that biblical figures were no saints, not even Abraham, the so-called father of believers. They were ordinary human beings with their good and bad sides, their strengths and weaknesses, and each lived at a particular time in history and in a particular culture with its imperfect customs.

Becoming fully human

The Bible, therefore, is neither a theology manual answering delicate moral questions nor a list of virtues and saints to imitate. But if that's the case, how can we turn to the Bible for guidance? Or, more specifically, what is it that we should be looking for?

Quite simply, the answer is this — the Bible contains a number of fundamental life principles, life attitudes and deep human values which transcend time and culture. These principles provide no ready answers to specific questions, but they do point us in a certain direction. The Bible depicts a life ideal. Each culture, each generation, each individual must therefore discover how to apply these principles to live biblically.

No single biblical book contains all these life principles. Each gives only a limited picture. Indeed, one book may add to, or even correct, what was presented in a very incomplete way in another book. Only the Bible in its totality is "canonical," a term which comes from the Greek word meaning "norm" or "rule" of faith. This means no one book, no section of a book, is sufficient unto itself. Only the whole Bible is normative for the believing community.

And the Bible is very clear on one point — no person is an island. We are only human through a triple relationship; namely, to God, to other people and to creation. To live according to the Bible demands openness to God, solidarity with others and respect for nature. In the three chapters that follow, I will examine each of these relationships and, in so doing, reflect upon what it means to become fully human from a biblical perspective.

Chapter One

OPENNESS TO GOD

* * * * *

For people in biblical times the existence of God was not in question. God is mentioned on every page and in nearly every verse of the Scriptures.

Neither far away nor difficult to reach, this God is very close to us. When Moses is sent to free his people from slavery in Egypt, he wants to know God's name. The answer is: "I Am who I Am" (Exodus 3:14). This is not primarily some philosophical definition of God's "being" from all eternity, but rather a statement about God's "being with." Yahweh, the special name of the God of Israel, implies that God is with us. Indeed, in revealing his name, God promises Moses that: "I shall be with you" (Exodus 3:12). God gives the same assurance to Joshua: "I will be with you as I was with Moses" (Joshua 1:5) and also to David: "Yahweh is with you" (2 Samuel 7:3).

God is with us! This notion is a refrain which echoes throughout the whole Bible, continually emphasizing that God and humanity are in a relationship. And it is in this relationship that we discover who and what we are. But this requires openness to God.

* * * * *

1. SEARCH

When it comes to life ideals or life principles we have before us a rich variety of possible choices. But how will we choose? What answers will we give to the many questions that life raises? If we desire, we can consult God. On nearly every page of the Bible you can probably find the phrase, "God said to..." People in biblical times didn't doubt that God spoke to them. Modern day people, in a certain sense, still say the same thing. Some of us believe that we are called by God, even if we've never actually heard a voice. But where do we find this divine voice that speaks to us?

People, nature and conscience

If we read the Bible carefully, we find that God speaks to us in many different ways. First of all, God speaks to us through the *people* with whom we live. The Book of Genesis states that God visited Abraham, but that the visit took place when Abraham met with three men: "Yahweh appeared to him at the oak of Mamre while he was sitting by the entrance of the tent during the hottest part of the day. He looked up, and there he saw three men standing near him..." (Genesis 18:1-2).

18

The people of Israel often heard the words, "Yahweh says this..." addressed to them. Yet, what they heard was not some mysterious divine voice out of the clouds, but the very human voice of Amos, Hosea or one of the many other prophets. And so it is with us. We, too, hear God's voice through the prophets whom the Spirit raises up in our world.

God also speaks to us through *nature*. This is well illustrated in the Book of Job. When Job loses everything and falls ill, he no longer sees any meaning in life. His theologian friends provide him with all kinds of theoretical explanations, but these confuse Job even more. At last, says the text, God speaks to Job (38:1-42:6). And what does God "say"? He starts speaking about nature and posing questions: Where was Job when God created everything? Is Job capable of imitating God? There is a plan and an order to nature, and in making this discovery, Job comes to understand that his existence and thus also his suffering are part of a divine plan and therefore meaningful. By looking at nature Job has heard God's voice.

Finally, God speaks to us through the interior voice of our *conscience*. This is how we can understand the many biblical stories in which God speaks directly to the person.

Who is this God?

Yahweh, Father-Son-Spirit, Allah — these are some of the names we have for the God who speaks to us, and the Bible teaches us something about this pluralism.

The story about the call of Abraham starts with the words: "Yahweh said to Abram..." (Genesis 12:1). This statement raises several problems. The Bible affirms explicitly that the name Yahweh only became known at the time of Moses (Exodus 3:13-14), and it admits without hesitation that Abraham did not know Yahweh: "To Abraham and Isaac and Jacob I appeared as El Shaddai; I did not make myself known to them by my name Yahweh" (Exodus 6:3). Elsewhere we even find that the family of Abraham adored many gods: "In ancient days your ancestors lived beyond the River — such was Terah the father of Abraham and of Nahor — and they served other gods" (Joshua 24:2). (Thanks to scientific research we now know that these gods were part of a moon cult.) Abraham thus could only listen to the voices of these gods, not to a god (Yahweh) he did not know.

Nevertheless, says the biblical writer, Abraham really did listen to the call of Yahweh in this way. By following his conscience Abraham actually obeyed the true God, even though he did not know the name Yahweh.

Many prophets, besides preaching to Israel, also addressed themselves to foreign nations. The Book of Amos contains a list of these prophecies against Israel's neighbours (Amos 1:3-2:3). All these nations are judged and punished by Yahweh, the God of Israel, a God totally unknown to them. Their crime was always the same: a lack of respect for their fellow human beings. (For instance, in Amos 1:6-9, punishment occurs ''because they have deported entire nations as slaves...'') Amos feels that all people know, deep in their hearts, that they have to respect their neighbours. This knowledge is engraved in the conscience of everyone. If people do not follow their conscience, concludes Amos, they commit crimes against Yahweh, even without knowing him.

The point that Amos was making is equally valid today. Even people who claim not to believe in God are obliged to make life choices, and they too must listen to three distinct voices: those of their fellow human beings, of nature and of their own conscience. Whoever listens to these three voices, listens to the voice of God, regardless of the name one gives to this God or even if one denies God's existence.

Conflicting voices

To be open to God in this way may seem simple, but in reality it is much more complicated because we hear many different and sometimes contradictory voices. The Bible, in fact, contains several stories about prophets fighting each other, each one claiming to be a true prophet and thus deserving of the trust of the people. (Two clear examples are the conflict between Micaiah and Zedekiah in 1 Kings 22 and the dispute between Jeremiah and Hananiah in Jeremiah 28.) If prophets disagree and have difficulties discerning the true word of God, then, of course, it's not surprising that we have the same problem. In the midst of the many possibilities and contradictions, how are we to discern the true voice of God speaking to us through other people, in nature and in our own conscience? The stories of Job and Samuel are helpful in this regard.

After Job has listened to all the beautiful theories of his theologian friends without arriving at a solution to his problems, he starts getting some insight by looking at nature. In this way Job has listened to God's voice. His conclusion is therefore very revealing: ''I knew you only by hearsay; but now, have I seen you with my own eyes'' (Job 42:5). Job has learned to *see*. He has discovered, perhaps for the first time in his life, the beauty and order of nature. He now sees in it a divine plan; he has come in contact with God's power and wisdom. He has learned to look, to see and to admire. In this way, Job has seen God with his own eyes. He has looked at nature and thus discovered God.

The Bible states explicitly that we cannot see God. To do so is to die! On the other hand, to hear God's voice speaking to us through other people or in our own conscience requires that we learn to *listen*.

The story of the call of Samuel (1 Samuel 3) illustrates this in a simple way. Samuel was sleeping in the sanctuary ''when Yahweh called, 'Samuel! Samuel!' He answered, 'Here I am.' Then he ran to Eli and said, 'Here I am, since you called me.' Eli said, 'I did not call. Go back and lie down.' So he went and lay down'' (v.4-5). This is repeated a second time and, adds the text, ''Samuel had as yet no

23

knowledge of Yahweh and the word of Yahweh had not yet been revealed to him" (v.7).

This is the description of a person who becomes conscious that changes are taking place in his heart. Samuel hears something, but he does not understand it. He goes for advice to another person who is equally incapable of providing clarity. After Yahweh speaks to Samuel a third time and Samuel once more runs to Eli, the old man begins to understand what is going on: "Eli then understood that it was Yahweh who was calling the boy..." (v.8).

What is beautiful about this whole story is that Eli refuses to make any decision in Samuel's name. On the contrary, Eli sends Samuel back and makes him realize that he himself will have to discover God's voice in his own conscience. "Go and lie down," he tells Samuel, "and if someone calls say, 'Speak, Yahweh, your servant is listening'" (v.9). Until now, Samuel had been running to others for answers whenever he heard something. This time, he follows Eli's advice. Upon his return, "Yahweh then came and stood by, calling as he had done before, 'Samuel! Samuel!' Samuel answered, 'Speak, Yahweh, your servant is listening'" (v.10). Samuel has finally learned to take the time to listen to what he hears and, in so doing, discovers God's plan (v. 11-14).

The stories of Job and Samuel say a great deal about the process of discerning God's voice. Job was open to God by *seeing* him in nature, Samuel by *listening* to him in his own heart, thanks to another person. To live biblically means to be open to God. This presupposes that we first search out those locations where God speaks to us: in another person, in nature and in our own heart.

Yet, our various activities, life's many pressures and our numerous obligations sometimes make it difficult to listen to God's voice. What is required is time... and courage. We might very well make discoveries resulting in personal dilemmas that can be resolved only by courageous and difficult decisions. Jesus spoke about this problem. It was not a new one, since Jesus used words spoken by Isaiah centuries before. These words are still valid for our age and, indeed, for all ages:

> The reason I talk to them in parables is that they look without seeing and listen without hearing or understanding. So in their case this prophecy of Isaiah is being filfilled:

You will listen and listen again,
but not understand,
see and see again,
but not perceive.
For the heart of this nation
has grown coarse,
their ears are dull of hearing,
and they shut their eyes,
for fear they should
see with their eyes,
hear with their ears,
understand with their heart,
and be converted
and be healed by me.

But happy are your eyes because they see, your ears because they hear! (Matthew 13:13-16; cf Isaiah 6:9-11)

2. ACCEPTANCE

To search for God's voice and to discover thereby the meaning of our own existence and life options are insufficient. To *know* is not enough — we must be ready to *accept*. ''It is not those who say to me, 'Lord, Lord,' who enter the kingdom of heaven, but the person who does the will of my Father in heaven'' (Matthew 7:21). There are, of course, different ways of accepting what has to be done. Unbelievers can say that being honest with oneself is necessary. Believers will say the same thing. But they'll add that being honest with self means accepting God's will over their life.

Let us now turn to three different ways in which acceptance comes about.

Of course I will!

Some people reach a *spontaneous and resolute acceptance*. Several biblical stories illustrate such acceptance.

One very good example is the call narrative of Abraham in Genesis 12:1-9. The chapter begins with Yahweh saying to him: ''Leave your country, your family and your father's house, for the land I will show you. I will make you a great nation..." (v.1-2). Abraham listened to the voice of God. The choice was not an easy one, but he nonetheless said yes. He decided to leave the comfortable familiarity of his own environment in favour of the insecurity of the unknown. He chose to emigrate to a foreign land, and he continued to hope that he would become the father of a child despite his advanced age (Genesis 12:4) and the sterility of his wife (Genesis 11:30). His decision must have appeared foolish to his contemporaries, but he was undaunted. He searched and discovered. Above all, he had the courage to accept: ''So Abram went as Yahweh told him'' (v.4).

The life of the prophet Amos provides another example of this kind of resolute acceptance. While living to the south in Judah, Amos becomes convinced that he has a mission to fulfil in the northern kingdom of Israel. He must have known that the word of a southerner would not be welcomed in the north. Though his choice might seem pure stupidity, he nonetheless accepts the divine voice. When he gets into conflict with the authorities of Israel and is expelled from there, he affirms clearly why he came: ''It was Yahweh who took me from herding the flock, and Yahweh who said, 'Go,

prophesy to my people Israel'" (Amos 7:15).
On another occasion Amos describes how irre-
sistible God's voice is: "The lion roars: who
can help feeling afraid? The Lord Yahweh
speaks: who can refuse to prophesy?" (Amos
3:8; cf the whole passage 3:3-8).

But why me?

Other people, such as Moses and Jeremiah,
were capable only of *hesitant acceptance*.

Moses was an Israelite who, due to extraordinary circumstances, was educated at the court
of the Egyptian Pharaoh (Exodus 2:1-10). He
must have enjoyed a prosperity unknown to the
average Egyptian. This wealth, however, did
not close his heart to human misery and injus-
tice. Indeed, the day he saw how slaves were
treated (Exodus 2:11) marked for him the
beginning of a clearer perception of his life
ideal. By looking at and listening to these poor
people, Moses discovered what God desired of
him. Moses realized that he not only wanted to
free his people from slavery, but that he could
in fact do something about the situation. The
circumstances of his life had prepared him to
be the right person for this mission. "And
Yahwh said, '...so come, I will send you to

Pharaoh to bring the sons of Israel, my people, out of Egypt'" (Exodus 3:10).

Still, Moses is afraid and hesitates: "Who am I to go to Pharaoh and bring the sons of Israel out of Egypt.... Never in my life have I been a man of eloquence, either before or since you have spoken to your servant. I am a slow speaker and not able to speak well" (Exodus 3:11, 4:10). Moses knows quite well that his objections are a poor excuse to avoid the task. He is certainly capable, since he has Yahweh's assurance that "I shall be with you.... I shall help you to speak and tell you what to say" (Exodus 3:12, 4:12).

Moses continues to hesitate in his heart. He fully realizes what he should do, and he knows deep down that he is capable. Still, he wonders. Why not assign somebody else to the job? Why should he, Moses, risk his life. Why not his brother Aaron? "If it please you, my Lord... send anyone you will!" (Exodus 4:13) Finally, after all these hesitations, Moses accepts his life mission.

The prophet Jeremiah is another example of this hesitant acceptance. Jeremiah sees clearly what he should do in life, but it frightens him.

He finds all kinds of reasons to put this option aside, even claiming that "I do not know how to speak: I am a child" (Jeremiah 1:6). But in the end he accepts.

Even if people see very precisely what they should do, they can always find reasons to hesitate. They can say, "Not now, next year" or "I do not know it sufficiently yet" or "Why should I do this when there are others who can do it so well or even better." But like Moses and Jeremiah, when they know they should do something of which they are capable, their conscience will keep bothering them until they accept.

I really don't want to

Finally, some people come to *acceptance after refusal*. Persons who behave in this fashion not only hesitate, but consciously refuse to do what they clearly see as their duty. After a certain time, however, they finally change their mind and accept.

The story of Jonah is an excellent example of this attitude: "The word of Yahweh was addressed to Jonah son of Amittai: 'Up!' he said, 'Go to Nineveh, the great city, and inform them that their wickedness has become known to me.' Jonah decided to run away from Yahweh, and to go to Tarshish'' (Jonah 1:1-3). What Jonah had discovered as his life project did not please him at all. He therefore decided to search elsewhere for happiness. But this did not work out as planned. Instead of reaching his destination, Tarshish, he runs into a terrible storm, is thrown overboard, swallowed by a fish and vomited up on the shore. There, Jonah again hears the voice of God very clearly: ''The word of Yahweh was addressed a second time to Jonah: 'Up!' he said, 'Go to Nineveh, the great city, and preach to them as I told you''' (Jonah 3:1-2). Finally, having learned enough from life, ''Jonah set out and went to Nineveh in obedience to the word of Yahweh'' (Jonah 3:3).

The little book of Jonah is a beautiful fable with a deep vision of life. Jonah sees very clearly his life mission but he tries to find his happiness elsewhere. This leads him to disasters which finally bring him to acceptance, even if it is not with a joyful heart.

In short, accepting what God has to say about the direction of our lives is not always easy. Some people hear but do not understand; others hear and understand but do nothing; finally, some hear, understand and do. Jesus described these various reactions in the parable of the sower:

When anyone hears the word of the kingdom without understanding, the evil one comes and carries off what was sown in his heart: this is the man who received the seed on the edge of the path. The one who received it on patches of rock is the man who hears the word and welcomes it at once with joy. But he has no root in him, he does not last; let some trial come, or some persecution on account of the word, and he falls away at once. The one who received the seed in the thorns is the man who hears the word, but the worries of this world and the lure of riches choke the word and so he produces nothing. And the one who received the seed in rich soil is the man who hears the word and understands it; he is the one who yields a harvest and produces now a hundredfold, now sixty, now thirty. (Matthew 13:18-23)

Openness to God means to search for God's voice and, after discovering it, to accept it.

3. FAITHFULNESS

A person, even after discovering and accepting God's voice, does not become a static being. Life goes on. Changes occur. New problems arise, new challenges appear, new situations influence us. We have new experiences, some happy, others painful. As a result the choice of a life option is only the beginning of something that needs to be developed. Indeed, if we're not careful, we may even deviate from a chosen ideal.

This touches upon human faithfulness. In the Bible we find numerous instances where God invites people to return to a chosen life option. The beautiful verb *shub*, meaning to turn, return or convert, expresses this notion. The person who has strayed from his or her ideal has taken a wrong road. But one can nonetheless change and return to the right road. In other words, a person can convert. The stories of Elijah and Jeremiah illustrate very well this aspect of openness to God.

I am tired of it

Anyone who resolutely accepts God's voice hopes that everything will work out just fine, but life is rarely that simple. We need only look to the example of Elijah to confirm this point. After discovering God's will, he could not hesitate or refuse:

> The word of Yahweh came to him, "Go away from here, go eastwards...." He did as Yahweh had said; he went.... And then the word of Yahweh came to him, "Up and go to Zarephath...." So he went off.... A long time went by, and the word of Yahweh came to Elijah in the third year, "Go, present yourself to Ahab." So Elijah set off to present himself to Ahab. (1 Kings 17:3, 5, 8-9, 10; 18:1, 2)

Elijah's mission, however, is a dangerous one. His life is threatened when Jezebel, the wife of King Ahab, decides that Elijah must die. The beautiful story of the prophet's journey to Mount Horeb in 1 Kings 19 describes the struggle of the prophet to be faithful.

Upon hearing that Jezebel wanted him killed, "he was afraid and fled for his life" (v.3). Out in the wilderness, Elijah tells God that he has had enough of life. What's the use of fighting all the time for an ideal? He wished he were dead: "'Yahweh, I have had enough. Take my life; I am no better than my ancestors.' Then he lay down and went to sleep'' (v.4-5a). That he should be tired of life is understandable. But is it a fitting attitude? ''An angel touched him and said, 'Get up and eat.' He ate and drank and then lay down again'' (v.5b, 6). Passive euthanasia is hardly the answer! You have to go on eating! Elijah was tempted to take it easy and to leave the fighting to others:

> But the angel of Yahweh came back a second time and touched him and said, ''Get up and eat, or the journey will be too long for you.'' So he got up and ate and drank, and strengthened by the food he walked for forty days and forty nights until he reached Horeb, the mountain of God. (v.7-8)

Upon reaching Mount Horeb (also called Mount Sinai, where Moses and his people experienced God's self-revelation), he went into a cave to pass the night. Elijah listens once more, again searching for God's voice. He rediscovers God in the quiet of the desert: ''Yahweh was not in the wind.... Yahweh was not in the earthquake.... Yahweh was not in the fire... (but in) the sound of the gentle breeze'' (v.11-12). Elijah listens to God's voice in the silence of his heart. And God asks, ''What are you doing here, Elijah?'' (v.13). Is the proper place for a prophet the desert, or a cave? Elijah knows the answer very well; he can only object that a prophet's life is demanding and that his mission apparently has failed: "I am filled with jealous zeal for Yahweh Sabaoth, because the sons of Israel have deserted you... and put your prophets to the sword. I am the only one left and they want to kill me" (v.14).

Elijah had experienced discouragement and disappointment, but deep in his heart that same divine voice speaks again: "'Go,' Yahweh said, 'go back by the same way'" (v.15). In this verse the writer uses the verb *shub* to which we alluded earlier. God invites Elijah to turn himself, to return to where he came from; he has to convert. And so he does, "leaving there" as verse 19 tells us.

After this demonstration of faithfulness, Elijah's life continues to be a constant search for and acceptance of God's will. "Then the word of Yahweh came to Elijah the Tishbite, 'Up! Go down to meet Ahab....' But the angel of Yahweh said to Elijah the Tishbite, 'Up! Go and intercept the messengers of the king of Samaria....' And Elijah set out" (1 Kings 21:18, 2 Kings 1:3, 4). Even when Elijah realizes that he is again in danger, he remains serene. "The angel of Yahweh said to Elijah, 'Go down with him; do not be afraid of him.' He rose and accompanied him down to the king" (2 Kings 1:15).

I have been betrayed

Another example of faithfulness to God, and thus to self, is the life of the prophet Jeremiah. Unlike Elijah, who resolutely accepted his life ideal, Jeremiah was quite hesitant. He objects at first that he is still too young (Jeremiah 1:6). But after this intial hesitation, he courageously accepts his mission, even becoming enthusiatic about it. Later in life, Jeremiah still remembers the joy that he experienced in his work: "When your words came, I devoured them: your word was my delight and the joy of my heart" (Jeremiah 15:16).

But life's difficulties increase, and when Jeremiah reaches forty years of age he experiences the crisis characteristic of that time of life, the noonday devil.

A number of texts (Jeremiah 11:18-12:6; 15:10-21; 17:12-18; 18:18-13; 20:7-18) reflect this so-called Gethsemane of Jeremiah. The prophet finds himself alone and abandoned. He undergoes resistance and rejection and even feels abused. And he is suffering because of his life option:

I never took pleasure in sitting in scoffers' company; with your hand on me I held myself aloof.... Do you mean to be for me a deceptive stream with inconstant waters? You have seduced me, Yahweh, and I have let myself be seduced; you have overpowered me; you were the stronger. (Jeremiah 15:17, 18; 20:7)

Jeremiah is tired of life: "Woe is me, my mother, for you have borne me.... A curse on the day when I was born, no blessing on the day my mother bore me! A curse on the man who brought my father the news, 'A son has been born to you!' making him overjoyed" (Jeremiah 15:10; 20:14-15). He even considers abandoning his life ideal, saying "I will not think about him, I will not speak in his name any more" (Jeremiah 20:9a). He realizes, however, that running away is no solution; he can find rest and happiness only by being faithful to himself and thus to God: "Then there seemed to be a fire burning in my heart, imprisoned in my bones. The effort to restrain it wearied me, I could not bear it" (Jeremiah 20:9b).

Jeremiah learns that he has to put things in perspective. After all, his life could have been much worse: ''If you find it exhausting to race against men on foot, how will you compete against horses? If you are not secure in a peaceful country, how will you manage in the thickets along the Jordan?'' (Jeremiah 12:5). He also learns that he should not complain or accuse others about his difficulties; rather, he must return to the divine voice in his heart and be ready to convert: ''If you come back (*shub*) I will take you back into my service; and if you utter noble, not despicable thoughts, you shall be as my own mouth'' (15:19). In this way a person becomes a strong and worthy human being, one who is not blown in every direction by every wind but who is as solid as a rock: ''I will make you a bronze wall fortified against this people. They will fight against you but they will not overcome you, because I am with you to save you and to deliver you'' (Jeremiah 15:20).

The examples of Elijah and Jeremiah illustrate that openness to God implies faithfulness. In their preaching the prophets often invited the people to *shub*: to return to a chosen ideal in spite of frequent temptations to abandon it.

The parable of the sower also speaks about this. The seed sometimes fails to produce fruit: people give up entirely on their life vision, either because of the resistance they experience (Matthew 13:21) or because of their worries and preoccupations or the lure of material possessions (Matthew 13:22).

4. FREEDOM

Throughout the course of history certain individuals have listened to the divine voice so well, and attained such clear insights, that their choice and their living out of a particular life ideal have inspired others. Such individuals become spiritual leaders and founders of religions, sects, religious orders or pious associations. And their ideals, once written down, come to serve as guidelines for their followers. Hence the birth of laws, constitutions, customs and manuals.

Moses was such a leader, and he was at the source of the Torah, the law of Israel, which of course underwent further developments in later centuries.

When we look at the origins of the Hebrew word *torah*, we find a notion of law quite different from our modern understanding. *Webster* defines law as ''the binding custom or practice of a community; rules of conduct enforced by a controlling authority; also, any single rule of conduct so enforced.'' For us, therefore, law denotes obligation, binding rule, controlling authority. Torah, on the other hand, implies guidance, directive or instruction. The law in the Bible is considered a helper at the service of people. Ironically, we are called, thanks to the law, to outgrow the law, to transcend the law, to become free persons, open to God, and delivered from the fear and the slavery of the law.

The Bible gives us several concrete examples of people who have reached this level of freedom.

David transcends the law

King David was one such person. He danced in Yahweh's honour with the common people, horrifying those who judged his behaviour unacceptable. This was contrary to royal protocol, since a king was supposed to observe certain rules out of respect for his rank: "Now as the ark of Yahweh entered the citadel of David, Michal the daughter of Saul was watching from the window and saw King David leaping and dancing before Yahweh; and she despised him in her heart" (2 Samuel 6:16). Princess Michal therefore says to David: "What a fine reputation the king of Israel has won for himself today, displaying himself under the eyes of his servant-maids, as any buffoon might display himself" (2 Samuel 6:20).

David responds, and in his answer resounds the freedom with which he dared to transcend customs and protocol: ''I was dancing for Yahweh, not for them. As Yahweh lives, who chose me... I shall dance before Yahweh and demean myself even more'' (2 Samuel 6:21-22).

At the same time, however, David is a weak person who allows his passions to overpower him. He commits adultery with Bathsheba and, to cover up his sin, he makes sure that her husband Uriah is killed in battle (cf. 2 Samuel 11:2-27). But, whatever his faults, David is nevertheless great for admitting that he has done wrong: ''I have sinned against Yahweh'' (2 Samuel 12:13). When Bathsheba's child falls ill as punishment for David's sin (according to the theological interpretation of the writer), David again puts aside all the rules of royal protocol, much to the chagrin of some of his officials:

> David pleaded with Yahweh for the child; he kept a strict fast and went home and spent the night on the bare ground, covered with sacking. The officials of his household came and stood round him to get him to rise from the ground, but he refused, nor would he take food with them. (2 Samuel 12:16-17)

44

But in spite of the king's fasting, the child dies.

The customs and the rules of decency governing mourning now require the king to fast. But when informed of the child's death, David shows himself once more a free man:

> David got up from the ground, bathed and anointed himself and put on fresh clothes. Then he went into the sanctuary of Yahweh and prostrated himself. On returning to his house he asked for food to be set before him, and ate. His officers said, "Why are you acting like this? When the child was alive you fasted and wept; now the child is dead you get up and take food." "When the child was alive," he answered, "I fasted and wept because I kept thinking, 'Who knows? Perhaps Yahweh will take pity on me and the child will live.' But now he is dead, why should I fast? Can I bring him back again? I shall go to him but he cannot come back to me." (2 Samuel 12:20-23)

Life goes on, not by mourning about the past, but by looking to the future: "David consoled his wife Bathsheba. He went to her and slept with her. She conceived and gave birth to a son whom she named Solomon. Yahweh loved him" (2 Samuel 12:24). David did not worry about what people said or thought about him, nor did he concern himself with protocol and the expectations of his officials. He transcended all this as a free person, even if he also remained weak and limited.

Hosea subordinates the law

The prophet Hosea is another person who, by listening to the voice of God, dared to transcend the law in freedom.

God told Hosea to '''Go, marry a whore....' So he went; and he took Gomer daughter of Diblaim...'' (Hosea 1:2, 3). Why Gomer is called a whore is not clear, and there has been a great deal of scholarly discussion on this point. Whatever the answer, the marriage was no doubt the subject of slander and gossip about its impropriety. But such talk did not disturb Hosea — he had listened to God's voice and he knew that he had made the right choice.

Yet life still brought him disappointments. The marriage ended in separation: ''She is not my wife nor am I her husband'' (Hosea 2:4). And, of course, this must have renewed the scandal. How unacceptable a lifestyle for a prophet, a man of God! Is such a person still credible?

Again, Hosea remains undisturbed. In his heart he continues to love Gomer, the woman of his life dream. Perhaps the separation will prove providential, a time of purification. Reunion is always possible, and a deeper, more sincere love, purified by suffering, may result.

But there is one major obstacle to this hoped for reunion — the law:

Supposing a man has taken a wife and consummated the marriage; but she has not pleased him and he has found some impropriety of which to accuse her; so he has made out a writ of divorce for her and handed it to her and then dismissed her from his house; she leaves his home and goes away to become the wife of another man. If this other man takes a dislike to her and makes out a writ of divorce for her and hands it to her and dismisses her from his house (or if this other man who took her as his wife happens to die), her first husband, who has repudiated her, may not take her back as his wife.... (Deuteronomy 24:1-4)

After all, who would do a thing like that? ''If a man divorces his wife and she leaves him to marry someone else, may she still go back to him?'' (Jeremiah 3:1).

Hosea is torn between the desire of his heart and the requirement of the law. Yet he knows that God's love transcends all laws. And so, Hosea takes Gomer back because he realizes that this is really what God asks of him despite law or custom. Hosea returns to his wife in full freedom: "Yahweh said to me, 'Go a second time, give your love to a woman, loved by her husband but an adulteress in spite of it, just as Yahweh gives his love to the sons of Israel though they turn to other gods...'" (Hosea 3:1). The message is clear: love transcends the law.

The Bible may seem very legalistic for the laws are indeed numerous. Nonetheless, the freedom described above is also part and parcel of the Bible. Every prophet speaks of it, and a book like that of Jeremiah is filled with it. It is not enough to observe the law of circumcision; one needs the circumcision of the heart. The fact of having a beautiful temple is no guarantee of salvation (Jeremiah 7:4).

Jesus completes the law

Freedom towards the law is also a charac-teristic of Jesus' attitude and a feature of his preaching against those who want to make us slaves of the law.

Jesus warns us that the many laws about prayer and fasting may lead to formalism:

> And when you pray, do not imitate the hypocrites: they love to say their prayers standing up in the synagogues and at the street corners for people to see them.... But when you pray, go to your private room and, when you have shut your door, pray to your Father who is in a secret place.... When you fast do not put on a gloomy look as the hypocrites do.... But when you fast, put oil on your head and wash your face.... (Matthew 6:5a, 6, 16a, 17a)

Jesus also warns us that the law cannot determine what is clean and unclean: "Pharisees and scribes from Jerusalem then came to Jesus and said, 'Why do your disciples break away from the tradition of the elders? They do not wash their hands when they eat food...'" (Matthew 15:1-2). Jesus' response is very clear: what is clean or unclean is determined by the heart. "What goes into the mouth does not make a man unclean; it is what comes out of the mouth that makes him unclean" (Matthew 15:11).

Another problem with the law is the way that it divides people into categories of who is or is not decent, who is or is not acceptable. Once again Jesus transcends this practice through the law of love, which is freedom. When the Pharisees asked the disciples, "Why does your master eat with tax collectors and sinners?" (Matthew 9:11), they were really saying that such an action is highly improper. Jesus overheard the question and answered, "It is not the healthy that need the doctor, but the sick. Go and learn the meaning of the words: 'What I want is mercy, not sacrifice.' And indeed I did not come to call the virtuous, but sinners" (Matthew 9:12-13).

Jesus viewed the obligations about the holy place of worship, the cult and the sacred times in the same way. For Jesus the laws regulating these could be guidelines only; otherwise, they would hinder our relationship with God and with others. His attitude toward the Sabbath is a perfect case in point. A law must never put a brake on love. Jesus heals therefore — we could almost say, preferably — on this sacred day when "work" is forbidden. "So it follows that it is permitted to do good on the Sabbath day" (Matthew 12:12). "The Sabbath was made for man, not man for the Sabbath" (Mark 2:27).

This same principle applies to any law. Love demands that we transcend the law, that we go beyond what the law prescribes: ''You have learnt how it was said to our ancestors: You must not kill.... But I say this to you: anyone who is angry with his brother will answer for it'' (Matthew 5:21-22). This does not constitute a rejection of the law, but its fulfilment: ''Do not imagine that I have come to abolish the Law or the Prophets. I have come...to complete them'' (Matthew 5:17).

Openness to God demands attentive listening to the wisdom of the law, which indicates a direction. But we should never use the law as a substitute for making a personal decision — to do so would be a desertion of our responsibility.

We stand before God with our conscience to discover what the law of love, which transcends everything else, requires of us. To live according to the Bible requires the freedom of which St. Paul speaks so often in his letters: ''But now we are rid of the Law, freed by death from our imprisonment, free to serve in the spiritual way and not the old way of a written law'' (Romans 7:6). Or, as he put it in his letter to the Galatians:

> Before faith came, we were allowed no freedom by the Law; we were being looked after till faith

was revealed. The Law was to be our guardian until the Christ came and we could be justified by faith. Now that that time has come we are no longer under that guardian. (Galatians 3: 23-25)

*   *   *   *   *

To live according to the Bible requires *openness to God*. This is a summons to be honest with ourselves, to live in truth, to live authentically. The answers to the many questions which sooner or later appear in life, and the ideals that we pursue, cannot be found in books. We have to *search* out how we must live if we are to be at peace with ourselves and, thus, with God. Each of us has to listen to other people, to the world and, above all, to our conscience. When we attain clear insight we must then find the courage to *accept* it and to live by it. No life is without difficulties, but these can become an invitation to deepen our *faithfulness*. Laws cannot provide prefabricated answers to the complexities of life. We have to transcend the laws in *freedom* by the law of love. Love surpasses everything. It can never be fixed in rules because it is always reaching further. Living according to the Bible does not lead to a static and passive life, but to a dynamic and active one of fresh commitments and new discoveries.

*   *   *   *   *

Chapter Two

SOLIDARITY
WITH OTHERS

*   *   *   *   *

We are not only related to God, and thus to each other, but to other people as well. We belong to a particular race, live in a particular family in a certain country and continent, and are members of the united (or more often divided) nations. After the story of the flood, for example, the Bible makes a point of listing the peoples on the earth, the descendants of Noah's sons:

> These were Japheth's sons, according to their countries and each of their languages, according to their tribes and their nations.... These were Ham's sons, according to their tribes and languages, according to their countries and nations.... These were Shem's sons, according to their tribes and languages, and according to their countries and nations.... These were the tribes of Noah's sons, according to their descendants and their nations. From these came the dispersal of the nations over the earth, after the flood. (Genesis 10:5, 20, 31-32)

Let us now examine how each of us, as individuals and as members of "countries and nations," should live our relationship with others.

*   *   *   *   *

1. ADMIRATION

The Bible presents a very optimistic picture of humanity. Indeed, the Bible is full of admiration for the greatness of human beings. They transcend the whole creation.

In the image of God

We have a very special dignity because we — male and female — are created in the image of God: ''God said, 'Let us make humankind in our image, in the likeness of ourself....' God created humankind in the image of himself...'' (Genesis 1:26, 27).

An ''image'' is something that we can see and touch. (When I look at the statue of an important person, I see, as it were, the person whom this statue represents.) The biblical writer adds that we are also in the ''likeness'' of God. This word indicates an analogy, a similarity, a resemblance. Thus, when I see a person, I see God, but only in a certain measure, by analogy. This explains the duty to respect human life: ''He who sheds man's blood, shall have his blood shed by man, for in the image of God man was made'' (Genesis 9:6). Because each of us is the image of God, we are nearly divine: "Yet you have made him little less than a god, you have crowned him with glory and splendour, made him lord over the work of your hands, set all things under his feet..." (Psalm 8:5-6).

This greatness is not the privilege of the first humans, something that would be lost through sin. The dignity of being the image of God passes from one generation to the next. "On the day God created Adam he made him in the likeness of God" (Genesis 5:1) repeats the writer, who then adds: "When Adam was a hundred and thirty years old he became the father of a son, in his likeness, as his image, and he called him Seth" (Genesis 5:3). As the father, so the son. This likeness of God, therefore, is not the privilege of one person only, but of all humanity.

It's quite instructive to compare the accounts of the creation of human beings with those of the creation of plant and animal life. In the latter case, the biblical writer stresses the many kinds of plants and the many kinds of animals:

The earth produced vegetation: plants bearing seed in their several kinds, and trees bearing fruit with their seed inside in their several kinds....

God created great seaserpents and every kind of living creature with which the waters teem, and every kind of winged creature.... God made every kind of wild beast, every kind of cattle and every kind of land reptile. (Genesis 1:12, 21, 25)

But when God creates humankind, no reference is made to different kinds. Whatever the race to which we belong, whatever the colour of our skin, each of us is the image of God.

Members of the same divine family

God created only one kind of human being. To stress this fact, the Book of Genesis presents all human beings as descendants of Noah and his three sons. This symbolic language emphasizes that we are all brothers and sisters. The prophet Amos accuses certain nations of failing to respect other people, and he condemns them for this. Amos believes that everybody knows, in conscience, that it is wrong to hurt and degrade others whom he calls ''brother.'' Human solidarity was threatened ''because they have deported entire nations as slaves to Edom and they have not remembered the covenant of brotherhood.... because he has persecuted his brother with the sword'' (Amos 1: 9, 11).

This motif of "brotherhood" or human solidarity appears repeatedly in the Bible. In Isaiah, for instance, God says:

> Is not this the sort of fast that pleases me... to break unjust fetters and undo the thongs of the yoke, to let the oppressed go free, and break every yoke, to share your bread with the hungry, and shelter the homeless poor, to clothe the man you see to be naked and not turn from your own kin?'' (Isaiah 58:6-7).

And in Matthew's gospel this same theme is evident in several passages: "Go and be reconciled with your brother first...." (5:24); "In so far as you did this to one of the least of these brothers of mine, you did it to me" (25:40); "You, however, must not allow yourselves to be called Rabbi, since you have only one Master, and you are all brothers" (23:8).

Since we are brothers and sisters, we belong to the same family and we must all have the same father: "You must call no one on earth your father, since you have only one Father, and he is in heaven" (Matthew 23:9; cf. 6:9, 26, 32; 10:29). The fact that you and I are members of the same divine family emphasizes the unique dignity each of us possesses.

A fundamental equation

Jesus himself emphasizes our divinity in words which equate God and human beings:

> Then the King will say to those on his right hand, "Come, you whom my Father has blessed, take for your heritage the kingdom prepared for you since the foundation of the world. For I was hungry and you gave me food; I was thirsty and you gave me drink; I was a stranger and you made me welcome; naked and you clothed me, sick and you visited me, in prison and you came to see me." Then the virtuous will say to him in reply, "Lord, when did we see you hungry and feed you; or thirsty and give you drink? When did we see you a stranger and make you welcome; naked and clothe you; sick or in prison and go to see you?" And the king will answer, "I tell you solemnly, in so far as you did it to one of the least of these brothers of mine, you did it to me. (Matthew 25:34-40; cf. the whole text 25:31-46)

It is difficult to imagine a stronger statement about our dignity as human beings. The first words at the moment of creation tell us that we are God's image; the final words at the moment of the last judgment speak of a certain equality, an equivalence between God and us.

From a biblical perspective openness to God is inseparably linked to solidarity with others. One has no meaning without the other:

> We are to love, then, because he loved us first. Anyone who says, "I love God," and hates his brother, is a liar, since a man who does not love the brother he can see cannot love God, whom he has never seen. So this is the commandment that he has given us, that anyone who loves God must also love his brother. (1 John 4:19-21)

And when a Pharisee asked, "Master, which is the greatest commandment of the Law?" Jesus reiterated the same point:

> You must love the Lord your God with all your heart, with all your soul, and with all your mind. This is the greatest and the first commandment. The second resembles it: You must love your neighbour as yourself. On these two commandments hang the whole Law, and the prophets also. (Matthew 22:36-40)

2. UNDERSTANDING

There are no essentially different kinds of human beings, only one humankind in which all are equal. Yet each individual lives this human dignity in a very unique and specific way. And so, each person is also very different from all others.

Differences point to limitations. The person who is tall is not short. You cannot be tall and short at the same time. All of us have our own richness and limits. The person who is short may dream of becoming tall, but that does not make the person tall. To live according to the Bible means to accept ourselves as we are and others as they are. We must learn to understand others and to realize that limitations are not necessarily defects.

Neither God nor complete

Human limitations are very numerous. The first fundamental limit we experience is being neither all-powerful nor all-knowing. Even if the Bible speaks of an equivalence between humanity and God, there is no complete equality. We may have everything in the divine garden of Eden, but this does not confer the right to eat of the tree of good and evil (Genesis 2:17a), which represents precisely this knowledge and power over eveything. A person possessing these would in fact be God and would thus cease to be human, "for on the day you eat of it you shall most surely die" (Genesis 2:17b).

A second fundamental limitation is that one is either a man or a woman, that is, a member of a sexual group that constitutes only half of humankind. After creating 'adam, which means simply a person (Genesis 2:7), God admits that this creature is incomplete. It is not good for a person — a man or a woman — to be alone. The one needs the other to become fully human (Genesis 2:18). So Yahweh divides humankind into "man" ('ish) and "woman" ('ishah) (Genesis 2:21-24). Both are clearly of the same nature and, therefore, equal (cf. also Genesis 1:27). At the same time, both are different and, therefore, limited. They need each other.

The biblical writer adds: "Now both of them were naked, the man and his wife, but they felt no shame in front of each other" (Genesis 2:25). Nakedness here refers to these human limitations. The man and the woman are very conscious of two very deep limitations: because they are human, neither one is God, and each is only a half of humankind. Yet, they are satisfied with these limits and unashamed of them. The text describes the harmony that exists in this imaginative dreamworld of paradise: people are happy with what they are and have, and they accept themselves and others as they are.

But once people refuse to accept their limitations and begin to feel unhappy because of them, this harmony breaks down. They start dreaming of transcending these fundamental limitations: ''But the serpent said to the woman, 'No! You will not die! God knows in fact that on the day you eat it your eyes will be opened and you will be like gods, knowing good and evil''' (Genesis 3:4-5). After they eat from the tree, what the serpent has promised indeed happens: ''Then the eyes of both of them were opened...'' (Genesis 3:7a). What they discover, however, contrasts strongly with their expectations. Instead of finding themselves all-powerful as the serpent had foretold, ''they realised that they were naked'' (Genesis 3:7a). The limitations with which they had once been satisfied are now experienced as a painful humiliation.

The harmonious relationship changes to disharmony. They, who once stood in front of each other without shame and full of mutual admiration, are now ashamed of their limitations. At this moment the masks we wear to disguise ourselves are introduced: "They sewed fig-leaves together to make themselves loin-cloths" (Genesis 3:7b). Now they also hide in front of God (Genesis 3:10, 21). The mutual complementarity of which man and woman feel such a need, and in which they find joy and fulfilment, changes into mutual aggression: "Your yearning [sometimes understood as yearning for power] shall be for your husband, yet he will lord it over you" (Genesis 3:16).

Differences lead to disharmony

Besides these two fundamental limitations, there are many others. People in the countryside are shepherds and farmers: "Abel became a shepherd and kept flocks, while Cain tilled the soil" (Genesis 4:2). Some leave the countryside and become city dweller: "He (Cain) became the builder of a town, and he gave the town the name of his son Enoch" (Genesis 4:17).

People also have different occupations and talents: "Jabal was the ancestor of the tent-dwellers and owners of livestock.... Jubal was the ancestor of all who play the lyre and flute.... Tubal-cain was the ancestor of all metalworkers, in bronze or iron" (Genesis 4:20-22). And when we cross national boundaries, we meet people of different races, who speak different languages: "These were Japheth's (and Ham's and Shem's) sons, according to their countries and each of their languages, according to their tribes and their nations" (Genesis 10:5, 20, 31).

All these differences contribute to the total richness of humanity, provided people accept themselves and others as they are. But many people refuse to accept their limits and seize what the other is or has. And because of this, these same differences can then cause disharmony and violence in the world:

> Yahweh looked with favour on Abel and his offering. But he did not look with favour on Cain and his offering, and Cain was very angry and downcast. Yahweh asked Cain, "Why are you angry and downcast? If you are well disposed, ought you not to lift up your head? But if you are ill-disposed, is not sin at the door like a crouching beast hungering for you, which you must

master?'' Cain said to his brother, ''Let's go out''; and while they were in the open country, Cain set on his brother Abel and killed him. (Genesis 4:4-8)

The law of the strongest now replaces understanding of the other. When Lamech, a descendant of Cain, has access to iron (Genesis 4:22), he can hit even harder. Lamech brags ferociously: ''I killed a man for wounding me, a boy for striking me. Sevenfold vengeance is taken for Cain, but seventy-sevenfold for Lamech'' (Genesis 4:23-24).

To go through every book of the Bible for a full picture of this disharmony is superfluous. The first book, Genesis, tells us that people do not understand each other any more (11:1-9), and the second, Exodus, recounts in the first chapter how some people make other people their slaves. We fight and kill one another, sometimes trying to justify such actions by calling them a ''holy war''! The historical books of the Bible are full of this.

3. RECONCILIATION

To re-establish harmony, we need to go back to our original place and stop trying to be someone else. And so, the theme of return and conversion reappears.

A certain refrain resounds throughout the Bible, and it stresses that those who exalt themselves will be humiliated. In the Magnificat, for instance, we read: ''…he has routed the proud of heart. He has pulled down princes from their thrones and exalted the lowly'' (Luke 1:51-52; cf. the whole Magnificat, Luke 1:46-55). And in Ezekiel we find the following:

> I will bring the Egyptian captives back and reinstal them in the land of Pathros, the land they came from. There they will constitute a weak kingdom. Egypt will be the weakest of kingdoms and no longer dominate other nations; I shall reduce her, and she will not rule any more over the nations…. And men will learn that I am the Lord Yahweh. (Ezekiel 29:14-16)

The message is clear: we must rediscover that our happiness depends upon being content with who we are and what we have.

Justice above all

Jealousy of what others are or have leads to violence and oppression. This has to change into a respect for others which lets them be who they are and possess what is rightly theirs. Justice is the only way to reinstall peace in a world of violence. It is also the first requirement for finding peace in our own hearts.

The prophets are the great proponents of this need for justice. Nothing, neither prayer nor religious practice, can replace or compensate for justice. Solidarity with others is the only way to achieve openness to God. It cannot be found the other way around. Justice comes first.

Consider the four following texts. They are among the strongest in the Bible. Virtually self-explanatory, they stand on their own and require no further comment.

I hate and despise your feasts,
I take no pleasure
in your solemn festivals.
When you offer me holocausts,
I reject your oblations,
and refuse to look
at your sacrifices of fattened cattle.
Let me have no more

the din of your chanting,
no more of your strumming on harps.
But let justice flow like water,
and integrity like an unfailing stream.
(Amos 5:21-24)

What are your endless sacrifices to me?
says Yahweh.
I am sick of holocausts of rams
and the fat of calves.
The blood of bulls and of goats
revolts me.
When you come
to present yourselves before me,
who asked you to trample over my courts?
Bring me your worthless offerings no more,
the smoke of them fills me with disgust.
New Moons, sabbaths, assemblies —
I cannot endure festival and solemnity.
Your New Moons and your pilgrimages
I hate with all my soul.
They lie heavy on me,
I am tired of bearing them.
When you stretch out your hands
I turn my eyes away.
You may multiply your prayers,
I shall not listen.
Your hands are covered with blood,
wash, make yourselves clean.
Take your wrong-doing out of my sight.
Cease to do evil.

Learn to do good,
search for justice,
help the oppressed,
be just to the orphan,
plead for the widow.
(Isaiah 1:11-17)

—With what gifts shall I come
into Yahweh's presence
and bow down before God on high?
Shall I come with holocausts,
with calves one year old?
Will he be pleased
with rams by the thousand,
with libations of oil in torrents?
Must I give my first-born
for what I have done wrong,
the fruit of my body for my own sin?
— What is good
has been explained to you, man;
this is what Yahweh asks of you:
only this, to act justly,
to love tenderly
and to walk humbly with your God.
(Micah 6:6-8)

Are you more of a king
for outrivalling others with cedar?
Your father ate and drank, like you,
but he practised honesty and integrity,
so all went well for him.

He used to examine
the cases of the poor and needy,
then all went well.
Is that not what it means to know me?
(Jeremiah 22:15-16)

Like his predecessors the prophets, Jesus also demands justice first. Clearly, there can be no substitute for justice. As Jesus reminds us, ''If you are bringing your offering to the altar and there remember that your brother has something against you, leave your offering there before the altar, go and be reconciled with your brother first, and then come back and present your offering'' (Matthew 5:23-24).

This demand for reconciliation, however, is only the first step. The person who has is also expected to share with those who do not have. This principle is well expressed in the following passages:

I cannot say that you have done well in holding meetings that do you more harm than good. In the first place, I hear that when you all come together as a community, there are separate factions among you.... The point is, when you hold these meetings, it is not the Lord's Supper that you are eating, since when the time comes to eat, everyone is in such a hurry to start his own supper that one person goes hungry while another is getting drunk.... (1 Corinthians 11: 17-21; cf entire passage, 11:17-34)

The whole group of believers was united, heart and soul; no one claimed for his own use anything that he had, as everything they owned was held in common.... None of their members was ever in want, as all those who owned land or houses would sell them, and bring the money for them, to present it to the apostles; it was then distributed to any members who might be in need. (Acts 4:32, 34-35)

* * * * *

To live according to the Bible implies *solidarity with our fellow human beings*. Real openness to God is impossible if we ignore the dignity of others. Solidarity means that we recognize the unique value of each person, that we stand in *admiration* of the human being. It also means that we arrive at an *understanding* of the person as a unique being characterized by both limitations and richness. The refusal to accept ourselves and others as we are leads to discord and oppression. The only way to restore harmony is through *reconciliation* based on justice.

* * * * *

Chapter Three

RESPECT
FOR NATURE

*   *   *   *   *

People in biblical times were quite conscious of their relationship with God and with each other. They were also very aware of being part of the natural world in which they lived. But their perception of the world was limited: they knew their own village, their own country, and, occasionally, they might hear about foreign nations from travellers. Their image of the universe also differed markedly from ours. The Bible presents a flat and firmly established earth, with a dome to separate the waters above from the waters below. Yet we know that the earth is a globe turning around the sun. Unlike today, the people of that time had no scientific theories regarding such things as evolution.

But the Bible does have very clear views on how we are part of the universe. Its insights can inspire us as we become increasingly aware of how we have neglected this aspect of our being human. Ecological problems remind us, sometimes in dramatic ways, that we are an integral part of the universe. They raise questions about the way we use — or abuse — nature.

Let us now look at what the Bible has to say about our relationship to nature.

*   *   *   *   *

1. BELONGING

Even if the Bible stresses our unique greatness, namely, our equivalence with God, the
Bible also emphasizes that each of us is a creature, a part of God's whole creation.

The creation account in Genesis 1:1-2:4a
describes how God made the universe in six
days. The last work on the last day results in
the appearance of humankind. And when you
compare this to the preceding works of creation, the importance of human creation
becomes obvious. The text is much longer, and
only humankind is a result of divine delibera-
tion: "God said, 'Let us make humankind...'"
(1:26).

The biblical writer uses the verb "create"
(*bara'*), which has a very specific meaning.
Only God can be the subject of this verb, and
the result of this action is always something
special and new. The verb therefore appears in
several key positions in the text: in the title
(1:1); when for the first time life appears on
earth with the creation of the animals (1:21);
with the creation of God's masterpiece, the
human being, when the verb is repeated three
times: "God created man (humanity) in the

image of himself, in the image of God he created them, male and female he created them'' (1:27); and, finally, in the conclusion of the whole account (2:4a). However great we as human beings may be, we remain creatures. We are not outside of creation; on the contrary, we are necessarily part of it, and belong to it. This fact is especially visible in our relationship to the earth and the animals.

No life without the soil

Human beings first of all belong to the earth, to the soil, to the land. The Bible presents this symbolically: ''Yahweh God fashioned man (*'adam*, which means human being) of dust from the soil (*'adamah*). Then he breathed into his nostrils a breath of life, and thus man became a living being'' (Genesis 2:7).

Whatever the scientific explanation of the origin of humanity may be, the biblical writer also offers a truth. We know that our bodies disintegrate and turn into dust; we can therefore conclude that our bodies are dust and come from dust. The wordplay between *'adam* and *'adamah* illustrates clearly how we belong to the earth. We not only originate from *'adamah*, but we also have the task of cultivating that

81

same *'adamah*: "Because you... ate from the tree... accursed be the soil.... With suffering shall you get your food from it every day of your life.... And you shall eat wild plants" (Genesis 3:17-18). In other words, the soil provides the nourishment necessary for our subsistence. Without it, life is impossible. And at death, we return to the soil: "With sweat on your brow shall you eat your bread, until you return to the soil as you were taken from it. For dust you are and to dust you shall return" (Genesis 3:19).

The land theme plays an important role throughout the Bible. Abraham leaves everything behind in the hope of finding land: "Yahweh said to Abram, 'Leave... for the land I will show you'" (Genesis 12:1). "Yahweh appeared to Abram and said, 'It is to your descendants that I will give this land'" (Genesis 12:7). Indeed, many of the stories about Abraham stress the importance of land: "When famine came to the land..." (Genesis 12:10); "The land was not sufficient to accommodate them both (Abram and Lot) at once, for they had too many possessions to be able to live together" (Genesis 13:6). And until Abraham buys a piece of land to bury his deceased wife Sarah, he remains a foreigner: "I am a stranger and a settler among you. Let me own a burial-plot among you..." (Genesis 23:4).

When the Israelites live as foreigners and slaves in Egypt, they also dream of having their own land: "I mean to deliver them out of the hands of the Egyptians and bring them up out of that land to a land rich and broad, a land where milk and honey flow..." (Exodus 3:8). And, indeed, their dreams will one day come true: "Rise — it is time — and cross the Jordan here, you and all this people with you, into the land which I am giving the sons of Israel" (Joshua 1:2)

It is a terrible tragedy when Israel (a word which may refer to the people as well as to the land) loses its land and has to go into exile and live in the diaspora. But even there, the people continue to dream of returning to their own land: "The Lord Yahweh says this: I will gather you together from the peoples, I will bring you all back from the countries where you have been scattered and I will give you the land of Israel" (Ezekiel 11:17).

In God's plan each nation has its own land:

For I will give you none of their land.... I have

given the highlands of Seir to Esau as his domain.... I will give you none of his (Moab's) land. I have given Ar into the possession of the sons of Lot.... I will give you none of the land belonging to the sons of Ammon. I have given it to the sons of Lot as their domain. (Deuteronomy 2:5, 9, 19)

We need land, earth, soil; without it we cannot survive. We are completely bound to it. We belong to it.

Similar to the animals

Animals, with which we share the earth, remind us how much we are part of creation. When we see a person, we see the image of God. At the same time we can also see this person's likeness in the world of the animals.

Animals, too, are fashioned from the same soil: "So from the soil Yahweh God fashioned all the wild beasts..." (Genesis 2:19). And, like human beings, they also return to the dust: "Indeed the fate of man and beast is identical; one dies, the other too, and both have the selfsame breath.... Both go to the same place; both originate from the dust and to the dust both return" (Ecclesiastes 3:19-20).

The human limitation of being only man or woman ("male and female he created them") is equally visible in the animal world. But so, too, is the richness. Because humankind is male and female, it can procreate: "God blessed them, saying to them, 'Be fruitful, multiply, fill the earth...'" (Genesis 1:28). In identical fashion, "God blessed the animals, saying, 'Be fruitful, multiply, and fill the waters of the seas; and let the birds multiply upon the earth'" (Genesis 1:22).

2. DEVELOPMENT

We belong to the universe, but not just in a passive way. In fact, God calls us to collaborate in the development and growth of the world in which we live.

Responsible stewardship

The first task entrusted to us is: "*Be fruitful*, multiply, fill the earth" (Genesis 1:28). People can pass on the life they enjoy. Human beings can multiply.

The value of life and the desire to produce new life are very deeply inscribed in the human heart. The joy at the birth of the first child is intense: "The man had intercourse with his wife Eve, and she conceived and gave birth to Cain. 'I have acquired a man with the help of Yahweh,' she said" (Genesis 4:1). To be sterile is a terrible disappointment. But even then, the desire for a child, for new life, remains: "Now that I am past the age of child-bearing, and my husband is an old man, is pleasure to come my way again!" (Genesis 18:12).

To lose a child is one of life's most painful trials. This is the misfortune of Job, when all his sons and daughters perish (Job 1:18-19). Great, therefore, is the joy when a new child, who in a certain sense replaces the dead one, is born: "Adam had intercourse with his wife, and she gave birth to a son whom she named Seth, 'because God has granted me other offspring,' she said, 'in place of Abel, since Cain has killed him'" (Genesis 4:25; cf. Job 42:12-15). And to live long enough to see how life goes on from generation to generation is a blessing: "After his trials, Job lived on until he was a hundred and forty years old, and saw his children's children up to the fourth generation" (Job 42:16).

A second task entrusted to us is to *conquer* the earth (Genesis 1:28). We may belong to nature and the world of animals, but we are also above it. We are called to work the earth: "Yahweh God took the human and settled him-her in the garden of Eden to cultivate and take care of it" (Genesis 2:15) "With suffering shall you get your food from it (the soil) every day of your life" (Genesis 3:17). Not surprisingly, the first son of Adam and Eve becomes a farmer: "Cain tilled the soil" (Genesis 4:2). The earth provides us with all kinds of opportunities. Precious metals and stones abound: "The gold of this land is pure; bdellium and onyx stone are found there," and iron as well (Genesis 2;12, 4:22). And in the soil we can plant vineyards to produce wine (Genesis 9:20). In short, we discover more and more the importance of the earth: it contains treasures and we can use it to make things grow.

We are also higher than the animals: "*Be masters* of the fish of the sea, the birds of heaven and all living animals on the earth" (Genesis 1:28; cf. also 1:26). We name them: "The human gave names to all the cattle, all the birds of heaven and all the wild beasts" (Genesis 2:20). Our capacity for naming indicates our authority over the animals — we determine what place they will occupy. This is illustrated by the fact that Adam and Eve's second son becomes a shepherd: "Abel became a shepherd and kept flocks" (Genesis 4:2). So, too, did Jabal: "He was the ancestor of the tent-dwellers and owners of lifestock" (Genesis 4:20).

Being the image of God, each of us is a representative of God. We therefore have authority over the earth and the animals. The verb "be masters," which the Bible uses to express this authority, has been misinterpreted at times. It does not mean that we have had conferred upon us the right or the power to do whatever we want. The command to "be masters" is not a licence to exploit. The master is one who is at the service of others. Our authority is God-given, but it in no way includes the right to exploit this planet. On the contrary, we are to be at the service of the earth and all it contains.

And how are we to fulfil this function? Because we are not the Creator, but the image of the Creator — as it were, co-creators — we must find our inspiration in how God wanted creation to be.

Orderly, good and beautiful

According to the biblical account of creation (Genesis 1:1-2:4a), God clearly intended to establish *order* in the universe, and everything has a precise place. In the first three days God creates the different spaces, and in the last three days their corresponding inhabitants. For instance, on the second day God creates the waters and the vault, and on the fifth day the fish and the birds.

All biblical texts about creation stress how well God planned nature, and how wisely. This wisdom played a very special role at the moment of creation:

When he fixed the heavens firm,
I (Wisdom) was there,
when he drew a ring
on the surface of the deep,
when he thickened the clouds above,
when he fixed fast
the springs of the deep,
when he assigned the sea its boundaries
— and the waters
will not invade the shore —
when he laid down
the foundations of the earth,
I (Wisdom) was by his side,
a master craftsmen....
(Proverbs 8:27-30)

Or, as Psalm 147 puts it: "He decides the number of the stars and gives each of them a name; our Lord is great, all-powerful, of infinite understanding" (v.4-5).

What God created is also *good*. After each act of creation God evaluates the result. And each time the refrain is the same: "God saw that it was good" (Genesis 1:4 10, 12, 18, 21, 25). Only after the whole of creation is finished does the text conclude that it is *very good*. Everything is now complete: "God saw all he had made, and indeed it was very good" (Genesis 1:31).

But God is also willing to accept that his work is sometimes not perfect. After creating the human being, God admits that what he did is incomplete: "Yahweh God said, 'It is not good that the human should be alone. I will make... a helpmate" (Genesis 2:18). So God creates animals. But the human is not satisfied with these new creatures: "No helpmate suitable for the human was found" (Genesis 2:20). God accepts the human's disapproval and criticism, and tries again. This time God transforms the human being into a man and a woman. When these two beings find each other, we hear uttered a sigh of relief: "Finally!" (Genesis 2:23). Now God's work is perfect.

There is also *beauty* in God's creation. Nature is truly impressive to look at: "Yahweh God caused to spring up from the soil every kind of tree, enticing to look at and good to eat" (Genesis 2:9).

Only God's love for us can explain nature's goodness and beauty. Everything was created for us and entrusted to us. God knows what we need: "His wisdom made the heavens, his love is everlasting! He set the earth on the waters, his love is everlasting!" (Psalm 136:5-6; cf the whole Psalm 136).

91

God wisely put order in creation and lovingly made it good and beautiful. We, as co-creators, have to develop the world along the same lines. We have to use our intelligence to plan for order, and our hearts to construct a good and beautiful world. We have to take pride in what we do, never being satisfied with mediocrity, but always striving for the best.

Our work, too, has to be complete.

3. PRESERVATION

Once, disappointed with creation, God decided to destroy it. "I will rid the earth's face of man, my own creation," God said, "and of animals also, reptiles too, and the birds of heaven; for I regret having made them" (Genesis 6:7). God then caused a flood to happen and everything disappeared. But after seeing the destruction and realizing that nothing had been accomplished by it, God admits to making a mistake. God therefore decides: "Never again will I curse the earth because of man.... Never again will I strike down every living thing as I have done. As long as the earth lasts, sowing and reaping, cold and heat, summer and winter, day and night shall cease no more" (Genesis 8:21-22). Never again will God disturb the order of nature with such destruction.

Respecting life

What God decided never to do again is what humanity, the image of God, threatens to do. Because we have sometimes interpreted our role as "masters" over the earth as a right to exploit rather than serve, we have also caused destruction. Nowadays we are becoming more conscious of the dramatic consequences of such a misinterpretation and of the need to protect nature and the different species of animals. And none too soon, since we currently have the technological capability of totally destroying everything.

At the end of the first creation account, the writer describes the food assigned to humans and to animals:

> God said, ''See, I give you all the seed-bearing plants that are upon the whole earth, and all the trees with seed-bearing fruit; this shall be your food. To all wild beasts, all birds of heaven and all living reptiles on the earth I give all the foliage of plants for food.'' (Genesis 1:29-30)

The text portrays both people and animals as vegetarians. In this way the writer tells us symbolically that no life is killed, since life resides in the blood, and plants have no blood.

At the same time, however, the text expresses an important difference between animals and humans. Animals eat ''the foliage of plants.'' Once the foliage is eaten, the animal must move on to another place in search of more foliage. People, on the other hand, eat ''seed-bearing plants'' and ''seed-bearing fruit.'' Note the two references to ''seed.'' Only humans know there is seed in plants and fruit. Even if we eat the plants and fruit, we can still sow the seed to grow more. Thus we will find food tomorrow, and succeeding generations will also have a chance to live on this planet.

In the new creation, after the flood, God also gives us meat as food: ''Every living and crawling thing shall provide food for you, no less than the foliage of plants'' (Genesis 9:3). This, too, is symbolic language. It tells us that the world in which we now live is neither perfect nor peaceful, as the dreamworld of the beginning could have been. We may eat meat, but there is a limit: ''You must not eat flesh with life, that is to say blood, in it'' (Genesis 9:4). In other words, we must respect life and avoid all foolish destruction.

The need for rest

As co-creators, we also have to take care of ourselves, just as the Creator did: ''On the seventh day God completed the work he had been doing. He rested on the seventh day after all the work he had been doing. God blessed the seventh day and made it holy, because on that day he had rested after all his work of creating''

(Genesis 2:2-3). We have to work, but we have to rest and recuperate, too.

We also have to give this chance to the animals. The sabbath is such a day of rest for humans and animals alike:

> For six days you shall labour and do all your work, but the seventh day is a sabbath for Yahweh our God. You shall do no work that day, neither you nor your son nor your daughter nor your servants, men and women, nor your animals nor the stranger who lives with you. For in six days Yahweh made the heavens and the earth and the sea and all that these hold, but on the seventh day he rested; that is why Yahweh has blessed the sabbath day and made it sacred. (Exodus 29:9-11)

Just as humans and animals need rest, so, too, does the earth:

> For six years you shall sow your field, for six years you shall prune your vine and gather its produce. But in the seventh year the land is to have its rest, a sabbath for Yahweh. You must not sow your field or prune your vine, or harvest your ungathered corn or gather grapes from your untrimmed vine. It is to be a year of rest for the land. (Leviticus 25:3-5)

Such periods of rest put a brake on the human desire for more and more gain.

Nature, which we have damaged and polluted, is in need of restoration:

The whole of creation is eagerly waiting for God to reveal his sons. It was not for any fault on the part of creation that it was made unable to attain its purpose, it was made so by God; but creation still retains the hope of being freed, like us, from its slavery to decadence, to enjoy the same freedom and glory as the children of God. From the beginning till now the entire creation, as we know, has been groaning in one great act of giving birth. (Romans 8:19-22)

* * * * *

To live according to the Bible implies *respect for nature*. That's because we human beings *belong* to the earth, to creation. We are an integral part of it. What we do or don't do with nature has consequences for us. We have the power to *develop* our world, and we must use this power to serve, not to exploit. Creation, which God entrusted to us, is under our *protection*. We are therefore expected to ensure a healthy existence for ourselves as well as a future for our descendants. We have an obligation towards future generations because we conceived and brought into the world the children who will make up these generations.

* * * * *

CONCLUSION

In this study I attempted to demonstrate that the Bible is not a manual of moral theology which provides concrete, universally applicable answers to each and every moral question that life poses. I also argued against our holding up biblical characters as universally valid models of how we ought to live, since each of them was human and, therefore, imperfect. Instead, I simply tried to identify a certain number of important life principles and life values.

I started at the centre, with the human being, since this is the only being we humans can experience from within. Whatever is outside of us is always seen through, and mediated by, our experience. We live with hopes and expectations, with disappointments and deceptions. We live with joy and pain. And we live with one another. No one is an island. Indeed, we are human only through relationships.

In our study we discovered life principles and values that point out what it means to become fully human. We did not find them in any one biblical book or in any one biblical character; rather, we found them in the Bible as a whole.

The biblical characters we met along the way lived some of these principles in their own specific ways, and at different times. These principles, therefore, do not belong to one particular period, nor are they historically conditioned. Indeed, they are still valid for us today.

Because these principles tell us what it means to become fully human, they are valid not only for Jews and Christians who read the Bible, but for all people. Anyone striving to be fully human can find inspiration in these principles, regardless of religious beliefs or lack thereof. The Bible does not belong to one particular group of people only; it is the possession of all humanity. Indeed, it starts with the story of humanity's creation (Genesis 1) and closes, in a certain sense, with the last words of Jesus (Matthew 28:16-20), which invite us to proclaim the good news to the whole of humanity.

The life principles enumerated in this study are inextricably linked to the triple relationship in which we live. To discover our own life ideal and to make correctly the frequent choices which life demands, we must be *open to God*. Or, as an unbeliever might put it, you must be honest with yourself. We are constantly in contact with other people. Whatever differences may exist among us, be they sexual, racial or religious, we must live in *solidarity with others*. And, as human beings, we are also part of the universe in which we live and find life. We must, therefore, have *respect for nature*.

If we cultivate this threefold relationship, and thereby strive to become fully human from a biblical perspective, life on earth will be good and there will be room for everyone.

SUGGESTED READINGS

The literature on the Bible has become very extensive in recent years. For any of you wishing to deepen your understanding of how to live the Bible, I would recommend the following books on biblical spirituality.

Bilheimer, Robert S. *A Spirituality for the Long Haul: Biblical Risk and Moral Stand*. Philadelphia: Fortress Press, 1984.
A reflection upon God's grace and the human response — in sin and in spiritual growth.

Dicharry, Warren F. *To Live the Word, Inspired and Incarnate: An Integral Biblical Spirituality*. New York: Alba House, 1985.
An overview of biblical spirituality focussing on the theme of relationship.

Osiek, Carolyn, ed. *Message of Biblical Spirituality*. Wilmington, Delaware: Michael Glazier, 1986ff.
This series of 15 books covers both the Old and the New Testaments. Written by scholars with your spiritual nourishment in mind.

Stuhlmueller, Carroll. *Thirsting for the Lord: Essays in Biblical Spirituality*. Edited by M. Romanus Penrose. New York: Alba House, 1977.
An edited collection of lectures and articles

which focusses on prophecy, liturgy and reconciliation.

Vogels, Walter. *The Prophet — A Man of God: The Interior Life of the Prophet*. Living Flame series 19. Dublin: Carmelite Centre of Spirituality, 1982.
A book on prophetic spirituality — the vocation, prayer, suffering and fidelity of the prophet.

————. *Reading and Preaching the Bible: A New Semiotic Approach*. Background Books 4. Wilmington, Delaware: Michael Glazier, 1986.
This book introduces you to a ''do-it-yourself'' method for reading the Bible. A study guide with exercises is included.